Baseball Inspired Python Tutorial For Beginners

JAE W. LEE

DEDICATION

To the bold dreamers and aspiring startup founders, and to the ambitious students who envision a future in software development, this book is dedicated to you. Just as a baseball player hones their skills through practice and dedication, you can learn the art of coding with this beginner-friendly Python guide. Fear not the challenges that lie ahead, for every coder and entrepreneur was once a beginner. Approach your journey with the same determination that leads rookies to greatness, and let this book be your steppingstone to turning your startup ideas into reality. May it inspire and empower you to embrace the world of programming, transforming your dreams into code. You have the potential to become a legend in the world of startups and software development.

With belief in your potential,
Jae   W.   Lee

CONTENTS

1

BATTER UP: PYTHON BASICS AND STEPPING UP TO THE PLATE

Hey there, Python rookies! Welcome to the first chapter in our baseball-inspired Python tutorial book. Today, we're stepping up to the plate to learn Python basics. So grab your bat and let's play ball!

Setting Up the Environment

Before we dive into Python, let's set up our programming environment. We'll be using MacOS for this tutorial, but don't worry, Python works on all major operating systems.

First, open your Terminal and type:

```
python3 --version
```

If you see the Python version displayed, we're good to go. If not, visit python.org to download and install Python.

Creating a Python File

Now, let's create a Python file. In your Terminal, navigate to a directory where you want to save your work, and type:

```
touch batting_practice.py
```

This creates a new file called "batting_practice.py". Open it with your favorite text editor, and let's start coding!

Python Syntax and Variables

Python has a clean, easy-to-read syntax. Let's start by creating a variable called "bat" and assigning it a value of 5:

```
bat = 5
```

In Python, you don't need to declare the variable type. Python figures it out for you. Now let's create a string variable called "team":

```
team = "Sluggers"
```

Printing Variables

To display our variables on the screen, we can use the print() function:

```
print(bat)
print(team)
```

Save the file, go back to your Terminal, and run:

```
python3 batting_practice.py
```

You'll see the value of "bat" and the name of the "team" printed on your screen.

Basic Arithmetic

Now let's do some basic arithmetic. We'll add, subtract, multiply, and divide using Python.

```
runs = 15
outs = 3

total_bases = runs + outs
print(total_bases)

strikeouts = runs - outs
print(strikeouts)

homeruns = runs * outs
print(homeruns)

batting_avg = runs / outs
print(batting_avg)
```

Save the file and run it again. You'll see the results of these calculations on your screen.

User Input

Let's interact with the user by asking for their favorite player's name. Use the input() function to get user input:

```
favorite_player = input("Enter your favorite player's name: ")
print("Your favorite player is", favorite_player)
```

Save and run the file. You'll be prompted to enter your favorite player's name, and the program will display it back to you.

Comments

Finally, let's learn about comments. Comments are lines of text that don't affect the program, but help us understand the code. In Python, we use the # symbol to create a comment:

```
# This is a comment
# Python will ignore this line when running the code
```

You can also use comments to temporarily disable a line of code:

```
#print("This line won't be executed")
```

And that's it! You've now taken your first swing at Python programming. In our next chapter, we'll dive deeper and learn more about variables and data types.

2

SWING FOR THE FENCES: MASTERING PYTHON VARIABLES AND DATA TYPES

Hey there, Python sluggers! Welcome back to our baseball-inspired Python tutorial book. Today, we're swinging for the fences and mastering Python variables and data types. Let's step up to the plate and get started!

Recap

In our last chapter, we learned Python basics like creating variables, basic arithmetic, and getting user input. Today, we'll dive deeper into variables and explore different data types in Python.

Numeric Data Types

Python has two main numeric data types: integers and floats. Integers are whole numbers, while floats are numbers with decimals. Let's create some examples:

```
innings = 9  # This is an integer
batting_avg = 0.325  # This is a float
```

String Data Types

Strings are sequences of characters. In Python, you can create a string using single or double quotes:

```
team_name = "Sluggers"  # This is a string
mascot = 'Slugger the Bear'  # This is also a string
```

String Concatenation and Formatting

You can combine strings using the "+" operator:

```
full_team_name = team_name + " " + mascot
print(full_team_name)
```

For more complex string formatting, you can use f-strings:

```
player = "Babe Ruth"
homeruns = 714
player_info = f"{player} hit {homeruns} homeruns!"
print(player_info)
```

Boolean Data Types

Booleans represent True or False values. They're often used in conditional statements. Let's create a simple example:

```
game_won = True

if game_won:
    print("We won the game!")
else:
    print("We lost the game.")
```

Lists

Lists are ordered collections of items. They can store different data types, including other lists. Let's create a list of team names:

```
teams = ["Sluggers", "Pitchers", "Catchers", "Infielders", "Outfielders"]
```

You can access list items using their index:

```
print(teams[0])  # Prints "Sluggers"
```

You can also modify list items:

```
teams[0] = "Home Run Heroes"
print(teams)
```

Tuples

Tuples are similar to lists, but they're immutable, meaning you can't change their values. Use parentheses to create a tuple:

```
bat_sizes = (32, 33, 34)
```

Access tuple items the same way as lists:

```
print(bat_sizes[1])  # Prints 33
```

Dictionaries

Dictionaries are collections of key-value pairs. Let's create a dictionary for a baseball player:

```
player_stats = {
```

```
    "name": "Babe Ruth",
    "homeruns": 714,
    "batting_avg": 0.342
}
```

Access and modify dictionary values using their keys:

```
print(player_stats["name"])  # Prints "Babe Ruth"
player_stats["homeruns"] = 715
print(player_stats)
```

And that's it! You've now mastered Python variables and data types. Keep practicing, and soon you'll be hitting coding homeruns! In our next chapter, we'll explore loops, conditionals, and control flow.

3

PYTHON'S HOME RUN: LOOPS, CONDITIONALS, AND CONTROL FLOW EXPLAINED

Hey there, Python all-stars! Welcome back to our baseball-inspired Python tutorial book. Today, we're diving into loops, conditionals, and control flow to help you hit coding grand slams. Let's step up to the plate and get started!

If-Else Statements

Conditional statements allow your program to make decisions based on certain conditions. Let's start with if-else statements:

```
runs_scored = 5
runs_allowed = 3

if runs_scored > runs_allowed:

    print("We won the game!")

else:

    print("We lost the game.")
```

Elif

You can also use "elif" to add more conditions:

```
runs_scored = 5
runs_allowed = 5
```

```
if runs_scored > runs_allowed:

    print("We won the game!")

elif runs_scored == runs_allowed:

    print("It's a tie!")

else:

    print("We lost the game.")
```

For Loops

For loops are used to iterate over a sequence, like a list or a range of numbers. Let's loop through a list of team names:

```
teams = ["Sluggers", "Pitchers", "Catchers", "Infielders", "Outfielders"]

for team in teams:

    print(team)
```

Now, let's use a for loop with the range() function to count from 1 to 9:

```
for inning in range(1, 10):

    print(f"Inning {inning}")
```

While Loops

While loops repeat a block of code as long as a certain condition is true. Let's create a simple countdown:

```
countdown = 10

while countdown > 0:
```

```
    print(countdown)

    countdown -= 1

print("Blast off!")
```

Break and Continue

"Break" and "continue" are used to control the flow of loops. "Break" stops the loop, while "continue" skips the rest of the loop iteration. Let's see them in action:

```
for number in range(1, 11):

    if number == 5:

        break

    print(number)
```

This loop will stop once the number reaches 5.

Now, let's use "continue":

```
for number in range(1, 11):

    if number % 2 == 0:

        continue

    print(number)
```

This loop will only print odd numbers.

Nested Loops

You can also use loops inside other loops, known as nested loops. Let's create a simple multiplication table:

```
for i in range(1, 4):
    for j in range(1, 4):
        print(f"{i} x {j} = {i * j}")
    print("\n")
```

This code will print a 3x3 multiplication table.

And that's it! You've now learned loops, conditionals, and control flow in Python. Keep practicing, and you'll be a Python MVP in no time! In our next chapter, we'll explore Python functions to help you throw a perfect game in coding.

4

PITCHING PYTHON FUNCTIONS: THROW A PERFECT GAME IN CODING

Hey there, Python champions! Welcome back to our baseball-inspired Python tutorial book. Today, we're learning how to throw a perfect game in coding by mastering Python functions. Let's step up to the plate and get started!

What are Functions?

Functions are reusable blocks of code that perform a specific task. They help make your code more organized and easier to maintain. Python has built-in functions like print() and input(), but you can also create your own custom functions.

Defining Functions

To create a function, use the "def" keyword followed by the function name and parentheses. Let's create a function that calculates a player's on-base percentage:

```
def on_base_percentage(hits, walks, at_bats, plate_appearances):

    obp   =   (hits   +   walks)   /   plate_appearances
    return round(obp, 3)
```

Calling Functions

To use a function, you need to call it by its name and provide the required arguments. Let's call our on_base_percentage() function:

```
hits = 200
walks = 80
at_bats = 600
plate_appearances = 680
obp = on_base_percentage(hits, walks, at_bats, plate_appearances)
print(f"Player's on-base percentage: {obp}")
```

Default Parameter Values

You can provide default values for function parameters. If an argument is not provided, the default value will be used:

```
def greet_player(name, team="Sluggers"):

    print(f"Hello, {name}! Welcome to the {team}.")
```

Now, you can call this function with or without the team argument:

greet_player("Babe Ruth") # Will use the default team value
greet_player("Lou Gehrig", "Yankees") # Will override the default team value

Variable Scope

Variables defined inside a function have a local scope, meaning they're only accessible within the function. Variables defined outside functions have a global scope and can be accessed throughout the script. However, it's best to avoid using global variables and pass them as arguments to functions instead.

Docstrings

Docstrings are used to provide documentation for functions. They're placed right after the function definition, inside triple quotes:

```
def batting_average(hits, at_bats):
    """
    Calculate batting average for a player.

    :param hits: int, number of hits

    :param at_bats: int, number of at-bats

    :return: float, batting average
    """
    return round(hits / at_bats, 3)
```

Lambda Functions

Lambda functions are small, anonymous functions that can be used when a simple function is needed for a short period of time. They can take any number of arguments but can only have one expression:

slugging_percentage = lambda hits, doubles, triples, homeruns, at_bats: round((hits + doubles + (2 * triples) + (3 * homeruns)) / at_bats, 3)

Congratulations, you've now mastered Python functions and are ready to throw a perfect game in coding! Keep practicing, and you'll become a Python all-star in no time. In our next chapter, we'll learn how to catch errors and handle exceptions like a pro.

5

CATCHING ERRORS: HOW TO DEBUG AND HANDLE EXCEPTIONS LIKE A PRO

Hey there, Python MVPs! Welcome back to our baseball-inspired Python tutorial book. Today, we're learning how to catch errors and handle exceptions like a pro. Let's step up to the plate and get started!

What are Exceptions?

Exceptions are events that occur during the execution of a program when something goes wrong, like a syntax error or a logical error. If not handled properly, exceptions can cause your program to crash. By handling exceptions, you can ensure your program runs smoothly even when errors occur.

Try and Except

The try-except block is used to catch and handle exceptions. The code inside the try block is executed, and if an exception occurs, the code inside the except block is executed. Let's see an example:

```
try:

    num = int(input("Enter a number: "))

    print(f"You entered: {num}")

except ValueError:

    print("Oops! That's not a valid number.")
```

In this example, if the user enters something other than a number, the program will display an error message instead of crashing.

Multiple Except Blocks

You can use multiple except blocks to handle different types of exceptions:

```
try:

    num = int(input("Enter a number: "))

    result = 10 / num

    print(f'10 divided by {num} is {result}")

except ValueError:

    print("Oops! That's not a valid number.")

except ZeroDivisionError:

    print("Oops! You can't divide by zero.")
```

Else and Finally

You can also use the "else" and "finally" blocks in exception handling. The "else" block is executed if no exceptions occur, and the "finally" block is always executed, regardless of whether an exception occurs. Let's see an example:

```python
try:
    num = int(input("Enter a number: "))
except ValueError:
    print("Oops! That's not a valid number.")
else:
    print(f"You entered: {num}")
finally:
    print("End of program.")
```

Raising Exceptions

You can raise exceptions in your code using the "raise" keyword. This is useful when you want to enforce certain conditions or notify the user of an error:

```python
def calculate_batting_average(hits, at_bats):
    if at_bats <= 0:
        raise ValueError("At-bats must be greater than zero.")
    return round(hits / at_bats, 3)
```

```
try:

    hits = 200

    at_bats = 0

    avg = calculate_batting_average(hits, at_bats)

    print(f"Batting average: {avg}")

except ValueError as e:

    print(e)
```

In this example, if "at_bats" is less than or equal to zero, a ValueError is raised, and the error message is printed.

Great job! You've now learned how to catch errors and handle exceptions like a true Python pro. Keep practicing, and soon you'll be able to tackle any curveball thrown your way. In our next chapter, we'll dive further into lists, tuples, and dictionaries.

6
PYTHON BASE-STEALING: MASTERING LISTS, TUPLES, AND DICTIONARIES

Hey there, Python sluggers! Welcome back to our baseball-inspired Python tutorial book. In this episode, we'll be mastering Python's data structures like lists, tuples, and dictionaries. Get ready to steal some bases and improve your Python skills. Let's dive in!

Python Lists

Python lists are ordered, mutable collections of elements. Let's create a list of baseball players and perform some common list operations:

```python
players = ["Babe Ruth", "Lou Gehrig", "Hank Aaron"]

# Adding elements to the list

players.append("Mickey Mantle")

print(players)

# Removing elements from the list
```

```
players.remove("Hank Aaron")

print(players)

# Accessing list elements by index

print(players[1])

# Slicing lists

print(players[1:3])
```

Python Tuples

Tuples are similar to lists, but they are immutable. This means you can't add or remove elements from a tuple. Let's create a tuple and access its elements:

```
teams = ("New York Yankees", "Boston Red Sox", "Los Angeles Dodgers")

# Accessing tuple elements by index

print(teams[0])

# Slicing tuples

print(teams[1:])

# Attempting to modify a tuple will result in an error

# teams[0] = "San Francisco Giants"  # This will raise a TypeError
```

Python Dictionaries

Dictionaries are unordered, mutable collections of key-value pairs. Let's create a dictionary of baseball players with their positions:

```python
player_positions = {

    "Babe Ruth": "Outfielder",

    "Lou Gehrig": "First Baseman",

    "Joe DiMaggio": "Center Fielder"

}

# Accessing dictionary values by key

print(player_positions["Lou Gehrig"])

# Adding key-value pairs to the dictionary

player_positions["Mickey Mantle"] = "Outfielder"

print(player_positions)

# Removing key-value pairs from the dictionary

del player_positions["Joe DiMaggio"]

print(player_positions)
```

Working with Nested Data Structures

You can also create nested data structures, such as lists of dictionaries or dictionaries of lists. Let's create a list of dictionaries representing baseball teams and their win-loss records:

```python
team_records = [

    {"team": "New York Yankees", "wins": 95, "losses": 67},

    {"team": "Boston Red Sox", "wins": 92, "losses": 70},

    {"team": "Los Angeles Dodgers", "wins": 98, "losses": 64}
```

```
]
```

```
# Accessing nested data structures
```

```
print(team_records[1]["team"])
```

List Comprehensions

List comprehensions are a concise way to create lists. Let's use a list comprehension to create a list of team names:

```
team_names = [record["team"] for record in team_records]
```

```
print(team_names)
```

Great job, you've just stolen some Python bases by mastering lists, tuples, and dictionaries! These data structures are essential in Python programming, and understanding them will help you level up your skills. In our next chapter, we'll dive into Python classes and objects, so you can keep scoring runs with your code.

7

THE PYTHON INFIELD: CLASSES AND OBJECTS FOR A WINNING TEAM

Hey Python all-stars, welcome back to our baseball-inspired Python tutorial book! Today, we're stepping into the Python infield and learning about classes and objects. These building blocks will help you create a winning team of reusable code. Let's get started!

Python Classes

Classes in Python are blueprints for creating objects. They define the structure and behavior of an object. Let's create a simple BaseballPlayer class:

```python
class BaseballPlayer:
    def __init__(self, name, position):
        self.name = name
        self.position = position
    def introduce(self):
        print(f"Hi, I'm {self.name}, a {self.position}.")
```

Here, we define a constructor method __init__ and an introduce method for the BaseballPlayer class.

Creating Objects

Now, let's create some objects (instances) of our BaseballPlayer class:

```
player1 = BaseballPlayer("Babe Ruth", "Outfielder")
player2 = BaseballPlayer("Lou Gehrig", "First Baseman")
```

Using Object Methods

We can call methods on our objects, like the introduce method we defined earlier:

```
player1.introduce()
player2.introduce()
```

Inheritance

Inheritance allows a class to inherit attributes and methods from a parent class. Let's create a Pitcher class that inherits from BaseballPlayer:

```
class Pitcher(BaseballPlayer):
    def __init__(self, name, position, pitch_type):
        super().__init__(name, position)
        self.pitch_type = pitch_type
    def pitch(self):
        print(f"{self.name} throws a {self.pitch_type} pitch.")
```

Here, we use the super() function to call the parent class's __init__ method, and add a new attribute and method specific to the Pitcher class.

Creating Inherited Objects

Now, let's create an object of the Pitcher class:

```
pitcher1 = Pitcher("Sandy Koufax", "Pitcher", "curveball")
```

Using Inherited Methods

We can call both the inherited and new methods on our Pitcher object:

```
pitcher1.introduce()
pitcher1.pitch()
```

Encapsulation

Encapsulation is the concept of bundling data (attributes) and methods that operate on that data within a single unit (class). Let's add a private attribute (number of wins) to our BaseballPlayer class and create a method to update it:

```python
class BaseballPlayer:
    # ...
    def __init__(self, name, position):
        self.name = name
        self.position = position
        self.__wins = 0
    def add_win(self):
        self.__wins += 1
```

```
print(f"{self.name} now has {self.__wins} wins.")
```

Using Encapsulation

Now, let's use the add_win method to update the number of wins for our player:

```
player1.add_win()
player1.add_win()
```

Congratulations, you've covered the bases in the Python infield by learning about classes and objects! With this knowledge, you'll be able to create reusable and organized code for your projects. In our upcoming chapter, we'll explore more about file handling, learning how to read and write data to help you become a true Python MVP.

8

GRAND SLAM: FILE I/O AND WORKING WITH EXTERNAL DATA IN PYTHON

Hey there, Python sluggers! Welcome back to our baseball-inspired Python tutorial book. Today, we're stepping up to the plate with file handling, learning how to read and write data like a star player. Let's get started!

Opening Files

To work with a file, you first need to open it using the built-in "open()" function. You'll need to provide the file's name and the mode in which you want to open the file, such as 'r' for reading, 'w' for writing, or 'a' for appending. Let's open a file called "player_stats.txt" for reading:

```
file = open("player_stats.txt", "r")
```

Reading Files

Once a file is opened, you can read its contents using various methods. For example, the "read()" method reads the entire file, and the "readline()" method reads one line at a time:

```
content = file.read()

print(content)

file.close()
```

Or, you can use a for loop to read the file line by line:

```
file = open("player_stats.txt", "r")

for line in file:

    print(line.strip())

file.close()
```

Writing Files

To write data to a file, open it in write ('w') or append ('a') mode, and use the "write()" method. Keep in mind that opening a file in write mode will overwrite its contents, while append mode will add new data to the end of the file:

```
file = open("new_player.txt", "w")

file.write("Name: Babe Ruth\n")

file.write("Team: Yankees\n")
```

```python
file.write("Position: Outfielder\n")

file.close()
```

Closing Files

It's important to close a file when you're done using it to free up system resources. You can close a file using the "close()" method. Alternatively, you can use the "with" statement to automatically close the file when the block of code is done executing:

```python
with open("player_stats.txt", "r") as file:

    for line in file:

        print(line.strip())
```

Working with CSV Files

CSV (Comma-Separated Values) files are a common way to store and exchange data. You can use Python's built-in "csv" module to read and write CSV files:

```python
import csv

with open("player_stats.csv", "r") as csvfile:

    csv_reader = csv.reader(csvfile)

    for row in csv_reader:

        print(", ".join(row))
```

Congratulations, you've now mastered file handling in Python! With these skills, you'll be able to read and write data like a true all-star. In our next chapter, we'll explore Python's powerful libraries and learn how to throw some serious curveballs with your code.

9
PYTHON'S TRIPLE PLAY: MODULES, LIBRARIES, AND PACKAGES UNLEASHED

Hey there, Python all-stars! Welcome back to our baseball-inspired Python tutorial book. Today, we're exploring Python's powerful libraries, learning how to throw some serious curveballs with your code. Let's step up to the plate and get started!

What are Python Libraries?

Python libraries are collections of modules that provide pre-written code to perform common tasks, saving you time and effort. They can be built-in libraries, like the math and datetime libraries, or external libraries that you can install using package managers like pip.

If "pip: command not found" error occurs, run the following command to properly install the package installer for Python (pip).

python3 -m ensurepip --upgrade

Using the Math Library

The math library provides mathematical functions and constants. To use it, you need to import it first:

```
import math

# Calculate the square root of a number

print(math.sqrt(25))

# Find the sine of an angle (in radians)

print(math.sin(math.radians(30)))
```

Working with Dates and Times

The datetime library helps you work with dates and times. Let's see some examples:

```
import datetime

# Get the current date and time

now = datetime.datetime.now()

print(now)

# Create a custom date

custom_date = datetime.date(2023, 4, 11)

print(custom_date)

# Calculate the difference between two dates

date_diff = custom_date - now.date()
```

```
print(date_diff.days)
```

Fetching Data from the Internet

The requests library allows you to send HTTP requests and interact with web services. You can install it using pip:

```
pip3 install requests
```

Then, you can use it in your script:

```
import requests

response = requests.get("https://api.example.com/baseball/players")

data = response.json()

for player in data:
    print(player["name"])
```

Creating Data Visualizations

The matplotlib library is used for creating static, interactive, and animated visualizations in Python. You can install it using pip:

```
pip3 install matplotlib
```

Here's an example of how to create a simple bar chart:

```
import matplotlib.pyplot as plt

players = ["Babe Ruth", "Lou Gehrig", "Joe DiMaggio"]

home_runs = [714, 493, 361]
```

```
plt.bar(players, home_runs)

plt.xlabel("Players")

plt.ylabel("Home Runs")

plt.title("Home Runs by Legendary Players")

plt.show()
```

Great job! You've now discovered the power of Python libraries, allowing you to throw some serious curveballs with your code. Keep exploring and trying new libraries to elevate your Python skills. In our next chapter, we'll dive into web scraping and learn how to gather valuable information from websites like a pro.

10

WORLD SERIES OF PYTHON: FINAL PROJECT SHOWCASE AND BECOMING A PYTHON MVP

Hey there, Python MVPs! Welcome to the grand finale of our baseball-inspired Python tutorial book. In this final episode, we'll showcase a project that combines everything we've learned so far and build a script related to baseball World Series historical data. Let's step up to the plate and hit a home run with our final project!

Project Overview

Our project will be a Python script that fetches World Series historical data from an API, analyzes the data, and generates insightful visualizations. We'll be using the requests library to fetch data, pandas to manipulate and analyze the data, and matplotlib to create visualizations.

Installing Required Libraries

First, let's make sure we have all the required libraries installed. Open your terminal and run the following commands:

```
pip3 install requests
pip3 install pandas
pip3 install matplotlib
```

Creating a New Python File

To start our project, let's create a new Python file. In your favorite text editor or integrated development environment (IDE) on your MacOS system, create a new file and name it "world_series_data.py". This is where we'll be adding our code.

```
touch world_series_data.py
```

Fetching Data from the API

Let's begin by fetching World Series historical data from the API. We'll use the requests library to send an HTTP request and parse the JSON response:

```python
import requests

url = "https://api.jael.ee/JLEE/python_world_series"

response = requests.get(url)

data = response.json()
```

Here's a sample JSON response payload expected from the World Series historical data API mentioned previously.

```json
[
  {
    "id": 1,
    "date": "1903-10-13",
    "winner": "Boston Americans",
    "loser": "Pittsburgh Pirates",
    "winning_runs": 3,
    "losing_runs": 0
  },
  {
    "id": 2,
    "date": "1905-10-14",
    "winner": "New York Giants",
    "loser": "Philadelphia Athletics",
    "winning_runs": 2,
    "losing_runs": 0
  },
  {
    "id": 3,
    "date": "1906-10-14",
    "winner": "Chicago White Sox",
    "loser": "Chicago Cubs",
    "winning_runs": 8,
    "losing_runs": 3
  }
]
```

In this sample JSON response, each object represents a World Series game with properties like "id", "date", "winner", "loser", "winning_runs", and "losing_runs".

Loading Data into a Pandas DataFrame

Now, let's load the data into a pandas DataFrame to make it easier to analyze and manipulate:

```
import pandas as pd
ws_data = pd.DataFrame(data)
```

Cleaning and Transforming Data

Before analyzing the data, let's clean and transform it as needed. For example, let's make sure the dates are in the correct format and extract the year for each World Series:

```
ws_data['date']          =          pd.to_datetime(ws_data['date'])
ws_data['year'] = ws_data['date'].dt.year
```

Analyzing Data

Now, let's analyze the data to answer some interesting questions. For instance, which teams have won the most championships?

```
team_wins = ws_data['winner'].value_counts()
print(team_wins)
```

Creating Visualizations

With the analyzed data, we can now create visualizations using matplotlib. Let's create a bar chart showing the teams with the most championships:

```
import matplotlib.pyplot as plt

top_teams = team_wins.head(10)
```

```
plt.bar(top_teams.index, top_teams.values)

plt.xlabel("Teams")

plt.ylabel("Championships")

plt.title("Teams with Most World Series Championships")

plt.xticks(rotation=45)

plt.show()
```

Saving Data and Visualizations

Finally, let's save our analyzed data and visualizations to files:

```
ws_data.to_csv("world_series_data.csv",                    index=False)

plt.savefig("championships_bar_chart.png", bbox_inches="tight")
```

Executing the Python File

To execute the "world_series_data.py" file, open a terminal on your MacOS system. Navigate to the directory where you saved the file using the cd command, like so:

```
cd /path/to/your/directory
```

Replace /path/to/your/directory with the actual path to the directory containing the "world_series_data.py" file. Once you're in the correct directory, run the Python script by typing the following command:

```
python3 world_series_data.py
```

Press Enter to execute the command. The script will fetch the data, parse it, and display a bar chart visualization of the World Series wins for each team.

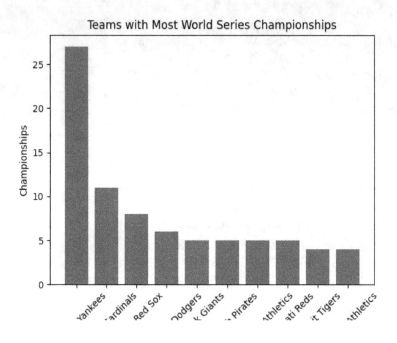

Congratulations! You've completed the World Series of Python project and showcased your Python MVP skills. We hope this tutorial book has helped you master Python programming and inspired you to create your own projects. Keep swinging for the fences and never stop learning. See you around, Python all-stars!

ABOUT THE AUTHOR

Jae Lee, Co-founder and CEO at Kempus, is a versatile leader with diverse experience. Prior, he served as the Lead Software Engineer at Cheil Worldwide UXD team, where he honed his technical expertise and contributed to the field of user experience design showcased through various global digital campaigns for Samsung. Throughout his professional journey, Jae has held various leadership roles, including leading RingMD, a telemedicine platform, and Quincus, an end-to-end supply chain visibility platform, as the VP of Engineering. He also demonstrated his innovative prowess as the Chief Technology Officer at WorldRoamer, an online travel agency platform for hotel and activities booking. In recognition of his exceptional contributions to the technology industry, Jae has been honored with the distinction of becoming a member of the Forbes Technology Council.

www.ingramcontent.com/pod-product-compliance
Lightning Source LLC
LaVergne TN
LVHW051623050326
832903LV00033B/4635